THE MORTALITY OF DOGS AND HUMANS

VICTORIA WADDLE

BAMBOO
DART
PRESS

LOS ANGELES † NEW YORK † LONDON † MELBOURNE

The Mortality of Dogs and Humans by Victoria Waddle

978-1-947240-62-9   Paperback
978-1-947240-67-4   eBook

Cover art by Dennis Callaci and Laura DeKloe

Layout and design by Mark Givens

For information:

Bamboo Dart Press

chapbooks@bamboodartpress.com

Bamboo Dart Press 031

www.pelekinesis.com

www.bamboodartpress.com

www.shrimperrecords.com

"One of God's great oversights is that dogs don't live as long as men . . . and that men don't move as fast as dogs."

—Sebastian Junger, *Freedom*

For the kind souls at Rancho Cucamonga Animal Center and Thrive Animal Rescue in San Diego as well as the City of Claremont for its foresight in maintaining a designated wilderness park.

CONTENTS

BEFORE FLETCHER AND ZAINY:
PONGO

When pregnant with my second son, I told my husband, David, that the kids should have a dog. My family had always had at least one while I was growing up. The truth was, I missed having a pup. As coyotes had moved into Southern California neighborhoods in the intervening years, I feared the fate of a small dog and focused on larger breeds.

These days, I see Dalmatians maligned online, but thirty years ago, I read books describing them as good with children. We purchased Pongo from a backyard breeder, a common way to find a dog back then. My three-year-old son, Matthew, named him after seeing the Disney cartoon. Pongo was gentle and persevering, just as my books had advised. Early on, I walked him regularly. I'd tie his leash to the stroller and off we'd go into the evening dusk, stopping to watch the sun set, Matthew reaching his arms out toward the giant blood orange and saying "Mine" while he tried to hug it out of the sky.

I entered a graduate program three years later, at the same time I was pregnant with my third son. I was already working full time teaching high school so my dedicated 'Pongo time' decreased.

We began to have trouble taking the most mundane walks. Dogs were often off-leash and uncared for in the neighborhood surrounding our first home. A pack of Chihuahuas escaped their yard on the regular and would bolt at Pongo, biting at his heels. Afraid he could easily rip one open, I would hold his leash tight and we'd make our way back to the house. Our next-door neighbors—who had once left for a weekend without arranging care for their cocker spaniel (we fed her by tossing kibble over the fence and running the hose on drip)—added a pit bull to their family. He broke through our wood fence and stayed, running back and forth into our yard for three days. We had to keep Pongo confined. Finally, I knocked on the neighbor's door and asked whether they'd noticed that their new dog was living in my backyard. The man who answered was in pajamas and clearly ill. He'd had the flu. But there were four other people in the house.

Though I was unhappy about the general atmosphere of pet neglect, my own Pongo routine failed when two incidents in my neighborhood scared me off.

One night I didn't make it outside until after dark. I'd already put the kids to bed and, feeling bad about Pongo's confinement, I decided to walk him around the block a few times. We passed the corner house when a Great Dane came racing out of the yard after us. I let go of the leash and the muscular Pongo took off like the proverbial rocket. David used to say he'd make a good wide receiver, always marveling at the way he could race and cut back, stopping on the dime and redirecting. Pongo outran the Great Dane, escaping harm. I thought I'd lost him, but when I returned home, hoping to search the neighborhood in the car, he was standing in the yard, waiting for me.

All that night, I couldn't sleep, thinking of what would have happened if I'd had the leash tied to the stroller. I ran the scenarios through my head. Pongo taking off and pulling the stroller over. My second son, Patrick, then three, head smashed into the ground, face scraped along until the Great Dane caught Pongo at which point a dog fight would ensue over Patrick, enveloping him. Pongo being torn apart by the much larger dog.

I was afraid to go out with Pongo again at night. Periodically, we still found time to walk during the day. My goal had always been to get away from the several blocks of houses surrounding us and head to the derelict vineyards adjacent to the neighborhood. Out there, we'd see a jogger or two, but no dogs bothered us.

On a spring holiday, I had the opportunity to walk with the stroller midday. I thought to go along the edge of the neighborhood and head toward the middle school, where, if no one was around, I could run with Pongo around the field a few times. After that, we'd go to the tiny park—really just a small sandlot—that bordered the school, and I could push the kids on the swings before heading back. I walked along the loose dirt edge of an abandoned vineyard, next to the street that escaped our neighborhood. On the other side of the street was the long block wall that acted as a neighborhood dividing line. Behind it were houses.

I'd stop on the drive home from daycare at a small park funded by the association fees of a neighborhood adjacent to ours, hoping no one would realize we didn't belong there. I continued to walk and jog when I could, but alone. After being bitten by a benign looking off-leash golden retriever—and then being threatened and flipped off by the owner after I said the dog had to be leashed—I carried a souvenir baseball bat with me, the eighteen-inch kind sold at stadium gift shops. Pongo's walks and time outside the house and yard were negligible. And while he regularly enjoyed playing with the three boys out back, deeply intrigued by their loading Tonka trucks full of sand and dumping it a few feet away, I felt persistent guilt, believing he wasn't getting the kind of exercise a dog his size needed.

When the youngest of my three sons, Alejandro, was six and Pongo ten, we grabbed hold of a brief window of opportunity, buying a house in a nearby college town we'd often visited, dreaming of living there as we strolled under the old live oaks or sat by any of the fountains in the many college courtyards. It had the quaint, sleepy look one finds in many areas of the country, but rarely in Southern California.

We all benefited from the move. There was a pool in the backyard. Patrick, who had suffered from allergies while so close to the country's largest diary preserve with its tens of thousands of cows and their tons of manure, now had clear sinuses. The yard was bigger. Pongo had more space. I walked him up and down the streets unmolested. I worked to make up for lost time and, while he had recently lost the ability to leap into the back of the Toyota 4-Runner on his own, Pongo was still happy to be on the move. A few months passed, and he turned eleven. I didn't think too much about this. The family dog we'd had when I was young, a twelve-pound terrier mix, lived to be seventeen. I knew big dogs didn't live as long, but Pongo was still muscular and active.

Seven months after we'd moved, Pongo had his first day of listlessness, leaving his dinner untouched. He'd never done that. Concerned, but not alarmed, I asked David to bring him around to the back porch, where I would give him some treats in his food and sit next to him while he ate.

Pongo came around the corner. Seeing me sitting on the porch, he loped toward me. When he was about five feet away, he stopped suddenly. His whole body convulsed and he dropped to the ground. I jumped toward him. His head lifted and, turning toward me, he snapped his jaw. I stood back, momentarily afraid he would bite me but immediately realized the snapping had been involuntary. I placed my hand on his side as he shook. I knew he was dying but I didn't want to call out, didn't want the boys to see this. It was all over in a minute, a thing I couldn't believe. He'd never even had a seizure before. Now he was still, his mouth open. His bowels released a bit of liquid. A few ants made their way to his eyes and I brushed them off. I went into the house and told David. After coming out to see for himself, we both went in to tell the boys. They came out to say goodbye. Both tearful and confused by their first experience of death, they didn't linger.

I thought of everything that was wrong with the situation—we hadn't had the chance to say goodbye, hadn't gone to the veterinarian since Pongo's last round of vaccines, couldn't prepare the boys or gather as a family while the vet instigated a peaceful crossing of the rainbow bridge. Now, we had a dead body on our hands, sixty-five pounds.

My first thought was to bury Pongo in the backyard, on the slope, to have him there with us. David dissuaded me from this. My fear of coyotes was still lively, and their presence near and among people had only increased during Pongo's lifetime. Our new neighborhood backed up to a designated wilderness area so we saw them in the yard, just outside the fence, all the time. What if one of them tried to dig up the corpse? Finally, David took Pongo to the vet, who sent him to the crematorium along with euthanized pets.

That night and for several nights afterward, I dreamed of Pongo. I was apologizing to him for not getting it right, not having the time to walk him enough, not giving him his best life. It's hard for anyone to have their best life when too many plates are spinning, but Pongo's happiness seemed a simple thing to stoke. He was loved and enjoyed family time, even if the consistency of his outdoor adventures sometimes fell through the cracks.

FLETCHER

Four months after Pongo died, we decided to get a new dog, this time from a shelter. The boys were growing and, having no more toddlers in the house, we thought we could take a chance on a dog with unknown qualities.

Again we were looking for a big dog who could spend time outside. I'd finished my second graduate program four years earlier. In the midst of a midlife crisis, I'd started training for a marathon. Pongo had been too old by that point to take on runs that often lasted between ten and seventeen miles.

David and I took the boys to a local animal shelter to have a look at available pups. The boys immediately fell for what looked like a vizsla (Hungarian pointer) because of her red coat. While we took her out to the play area, a woman on the shelter staff told us that "Ginger" had been given up because she had nipped and bitten in the past. Her owners had just had a baby and felt safety was an issue. As the shelter employee was relating Ginger's history, the dog turned and nipped six-year-old Alejandro. Just a nip, didn't break the skin. If there were no small children in the family, we could have worked with Ginger to end the habit. But with kids, she wasn't an option.

We walked the kennels again. A tawny wolf of a dog with amber-green eyes and a white arrow on his chest intrigued us. We went back to the front desk to ask for playtime. When the shelter employee brought us back into the play area, the dog ignored us.

We shook toys and little stuffed animals. He ignored those. His only interest was in whatever existed beyond the wall of the play area. He circled the perimeter, stopping to stand on two feet and see if he could stretch to the top of the wall.

"He's an outdoor dog," the employee said. "He's not very warm with people so far as we can see." She continued to warn us against him. I could see why. The dog, about six months old, had been neutered. Clearly someone had hoped to keep him, but he had escaped their care. I'd never known a dog with his sort of personality, so little interested in being adored. I began to see that, like people, dogs had neurodiverse personalities. And that this dog, who was looking to get going, just might work in our home.

"I'm training for a marathon," I said. "I could take him out jogging for miles every day."

We put a hold on the pup and went home to think it over for forty-eight hours. When we returned, the kids were excited. As we made our way home in the family minivan, the boys, who had been playing video games with historical themes, decided on the name "Fletcher"—after an arrow maker in the Middle Ages—for the white arrow on his chest.

The true nature of Fletcher's need to explore soon became clear. He wasn't a great climber, but he could pull himself over the four-foot gate in our yard. We realized we'd need a dog run with a six-foot wrought iron border.

Twenty years ago, I'd never heard of doggy daycare. The only way I thought I could keep him safe while the dog run was being built was to bring him to work with me, in violation of the rules. I'd started in a new high school library that year. It was still empty of books and even shelves. I spent most of each day either going into classrooms or hanging out in the textbook room with the two library technicians, where we cataloged and processed all the new books for the school. For a few days, I set up a bed in the textbook room for Fletcher, taking him on short walks during my half-hour lunch breaks, but also having to walk him in brief morning and afternoon spurts. In between, he stayed in the aisles between the textbooks, mostly content.

Once the dog run was built, Fletcher stayed home during the day. He slept in our house at night and also had a doghouse outside in case the weather got cold. Our lives in inland Southern California often include extreme heat, so we consider the few days that drop below fifty-five degrees as our winter. Fletcher didn't bother going into the doghouse, but he liked to stand on top of it for a better view down the slope, of the town below, and the horizon. He seemed to be forever yearning to be on the move.

Quickly realizing that Fletcher couldn't wait until I got home from work to take his run, I got up early on weekdays and took him for a walk before I left the house. As a school librarian, I routinely stayed at work a few hours after school to help students and catch up on desk tasks. While Fletcher was still a puppy, albeit one that weighed over sixty pounds, I left earlier in order to get the miles in before dark.

Soon after Fletcher came to live with us, we hired a gardener One morning, the gardener left the gate open. I didn't know until I got home from work, went out to get Fletcher for a run, and saw there was no running partner. With his energy and his power, he could have gone anywhere. I had just enough time to go to the nearest shelter, a vast outdoor facility, and view the dogs brought in that day. No Fletcher.

The following day I made my way to other shelters, including the one where we'd gotten Fletcher. The last shelter I visited, in the city adjacent to mine, was small and indoors. It was easy to circle through the rows of cells. I walked around the facility several times. Despairing and not knowing what else to do, I asked the front desk attendant, "Are there any more dogs anywhere?"

She said no, you've covered the facility. Then she asked, kindly— I thought it was an act of sympathy only—what my dog looked like. Though it really didn't matter at this point, I stayed to describe him. How he might be part husky, one of those warm caramel types, not the black, gray and white we usually saw in our area. His amber-green eyes, how we thought of him as a small wolf. And, of course, his white arrow.

"White arrow," she said. "Then maybe someone found him." She'd had a purpose, after all, in asking me. She reached into a drawer and pulled out a slip of paper. "A woman called this morning about finding a dog. She didn't want to bring him into a facility, afraid he'd be euthanized. So she called the local shelters and described him. He has a white arrow."

She scribbled the phone number for me. I thanked her.

Though cell phones existed, I didn't yet have one. I found a pay phone at a local market and called. The woman who answered listened to my description of Fletcher and said, "I think he's here with me. He has a leather collar, but not the tags you described. No identification." She gave me her address, a place not far from my house but directly behind the wilderness area where I would hike with him.

When I arrived at the neighborhood of condominiums that backed against the wilderness area, Fletcher loped out to greet me, happy as a clam at high tide. "You've been gone all night!" I cried, an observation that had no effect on his delight. The woman refused to take any payment for caring for him, saying she hoped someone would do the same for her. "He just trotted out from the wilderness." She pointed behind her. We both looked at the grassy hills, wondering. Not only were coyotes there, but my family had seen a bobcat and, more than once, bears. Signs at the entrance warned to look out for mountain lions. How I wished Fletcher had had a little camera attached to his collar. But then, he'd somehow lost his nametag and license. What had he done overnight?

I bought a new flat ID tag that slid onto the collar through two slots and was guaranteed not to break off.

Fletcher's need to be on the move helped me with my marathon training. We were out a minimum of four days a week and our mileage varied from the short runs at four miles and increasing up to twenty miles as the marathon date approached. In all this, Fletcher never tired. When my uncle, who had raised many hunting dogs, visited us from Pennsylvania, he said he wasn't surprised that a dog like Fletcher never wore down. "I bet he could go a lot farther than twenty miles," he said. I never tested this theory. The furthest we jogged was twenty-two miles. But if I was busy and missed any opportunities for outdoor adventure, Fletcher still looked for an escape. Twice he crossed a major boulevard. On one of those occasions, he entered an old folks home. Because his new ID tag was flat against his collar, the residents didn't immediately see it. They bathed him and had decided they would keep him before realizing he belonged elsewhere. Even with all our runs and the attention of the boys in backyard play, Fletcher needed something more. Maybe, I mused aloud to my family, he needed a companion to entertain him.

ZAINY

For Christmas 2004, David and our sons bought a Labrador retriever puppy, one that, early on, I thought of as a gift for Fletcher rather than me. I was having forty people over for Christmas dinner, and a brand new puppy in the house would have sent me over the edge. Thankfully, the breeder thought the puppy, who was a runt, too small to leave her mother before Christmas.

We picked up the pumpkin-colored pup on New Year's Eve. She was small enough to walk under her siblings. We named her Zanthe for 'golden-haired,' but her nickname, Zainy, was the only one she ever knew. She was comical but anxious, and no matter how much she ate, forever hungry. Like Fletcher, she was always on the move, imitating everything he did. I wondered if he was flattered as Zainy nudged her way next to him at the water bowl and followed his exact course of movement. Occasionally, Fletcher slipped through the gate but Zainy would only follow him as far as she could see home, seeming to fear the great unknown. Fletcher would eventually retreat to play with her.

Zainy had a heart murmur. I was afraid of running very far with her although she could walk a good distance after she was leash trained, a period in which she circled my legs repeatedly until she'd wrapped me mummy-style. Fletcher, who seemed to have made his peace with her shenanigans, would walk away to the extent of his own leash, circle and sit down, waiting. After we took our walk, I'd go back out for a run with Fletcher.

This continued for a few years, until my thyroid broke down, and I gained forty pounds in under twelve months. A work colleague, a PE teacher, told me that running on too much weight would blow out my knees. Fletcher, Zainy, and I began hiking more regularly in the wilderness area where Fletcher once was lost. There, Zainy pulled her usual antics, trying to gobble the grasses and chase lizards. Once, it was all I could do to hold her back from devouring a tarantula. Fletcher maintained his usual equanimity. He never shoved his face into the scrub to inspect the creatures therein. It was only Zainy who came home with ticks in her eyebrows and forehead. Single-minded, Fletcher always pushed forward to the next uphill challenge. That is, unless a squirrel crossed our path. Then all bets were off.

Early on, when Fletcher was a pup, I'd pulled him with me into the pool, under the disapproving gazes of my son who thought it was a mean stunt. "I need to see whether he can get out on his own," I said. He dog paddled toward the deep end and then, in a panic, scraped against the tiles on the side. Though I'd never seen a more graceful canine on land, Fletcher was no water dog. I pulled on his collar and he slapped at the water, moving in the direction I urged him, toward the steps. Once he was out, I pulled him back in with me again. I let go and Fletcher immediately paddled his way to the steps and out. That was all the reassurance I needed, and I never put him in the water again. Yet, once Zainy was part of the family, he periodically landed there.

Zainy introduced herself to the pool. During her first spring with us, on her first warm day, she put a paw into the water. And then another. And then she pushed off, gliding forward. Once fully in, she didn't dog paddle, but kept all her legs deep in the water stroking and pulling with her webbed feet, like the ducks that occasionally swam there. Though she was often ungraceful and goofy on land, she was an elegant swimmer. From that day forward, she glided into the pool in every season, her thick downy undercoat giving her the warmth she needed in the mild Southern California winters.

In addition to her heart murmur, Zainy had lousy eyesight, a fact made clear when she tried to catch a treat or a ball midair. She loved to run in circles around the backyard pool to work off some of her energy. If Fletcher happened to be walking near the pool, she would sometimes crash into him, sending him airborne and then into the drink. Poor thing. How he hated the water!

DOG V. NATURE

Whereas Fletcher lived to walk, run, and hike, Zainy loved a variety of things, top among them eating and swimming. She was shorter than the average Labrador retriever, so we committed to keeping her weight at sixty-five pounds. We had to separate her from Fletcher at meals because she would happily gobble up what was left in his bowl after she'd inhaled her own food. Bad as her eyesight was, she had a great nose and could sniff out lizards and rodents in the hedges, plunging her face into the bush to come out with some poor creature to munch on. Not infrequently, she would bound across the yard toward me with a mouse in her maw, the tail twitching in the air. Seeing her munching on god-knows-what, I often worried some terrible digestive ailment would be the end of her, but in her fifteen-plus years, she had tummy troubles only in very old age.

Zainy's need to put everything in her mouth periodically caused some embarrassment. Once on a walk, having had no knowledge of the Bullock's oriole, I saw what I thought was a dead Baltimore oriole on the side of the path. I'd never seen a Baltimore oriole because they don't inhabit inland Southern California. Just as I was wondering how it had died, Zainy lunged for it. The several other people on the path were taken aback, some stopping to watch the drama unfold as I tried to pry the corpse from her mouth. As newcomers passed, they seemed to think Zainy had killed the bird. A few said, "Oh my God," and "Gross." Afraid some virtue-signaling videographer would show the world what a bad dog mom I was in allowing my girl to kill another living creature, I got her to drop her black and orange bundle. It was unmarked, protected by the large soft gums that retrievers are bred for, but still dead.

During another multiple-day bird event, I was not so lucky.

Ms. Mallard was in the pool again. She had come weeks before with her iridescent partner, the pair floating through spring-sparkled water, creating a bucolic scene and an opportunity for me to idealize nature. Though earthquakes and wildfires are hard to put aside—my own neighborhood was aflame in the Grand Prix Fire of 2003—these vast catastrophes are periodic. Suburban Southern California is a mild place to live relative to most areas of the world. So the first time I found the pair in their limpid blue rectangle, my heart tucked into the presence of tranquility. That lasted until we found black stains on the plaster floor of the pool, the removal of which had taken a week of daily scrubbing with a long-armed brush. The "Mi casa es su casa" plaque hanging inside my gate didn't apply to these two any longer. I'd let Zainy out to splash down in the water, sending the ducks flapping over the wrought iron fence. Permanently, I'd thought. But here was the dingy brown female again—this time trailing six wispy ducklings behind her, their downy feathers fluttering like mini wheat fields in an imperceptible breeze.

Worried about the ducklings, I'd open the slider just enough to squeeze through and go outside. Inside Zainy repeatedly slammed the glass with her paw like an angry teen smacking a locker door. Thinking she'd crack the window, I pinched back inside and crated her. She howled so mournfully, I figured the ASPCA would be at the door at any moment.

When I tried to chase them away, I found the ducklings were too small to pop up over the tile edge and out of the pool. How odd that they were in danger of being stranded in what was their natural element. Raising the water level would take time. Better, I thought, to net each duckling in turn; but though they couldn't yet fly, they were expert divers, and under they went whenever I drew near. Looking for a bridge, I dragged a plank from under a camellia bush. It sank. I found a bodysurfing board that could both float in the pool at one end and hug the cement on the other.

Again the ducklings evaded me, zagging all ways while I tried herding them toward the board. After an hour, winded, liquid moons of sweat under my arms, I succeeded in getting Ms. Mallard out. The ducklings followed. As I stepped back, mom hopped in again and all six ducklings took the plunge behind her. They outwitted me in their folly, in their complete lack of backyard survival skills. I thought I might give up, but round two was much easier, with mom quickly up the foam board and over the fence, her ducklings easily popping between the iron shafts. Gone at last.

Hours later, I let Zainy out. She bolted for the pool, but immediately cut back right and jumped behind the red lava rock under the baby palm. Feathers flew. "Zainy! No!" She snapped her head once, and then dashed after Ms. Mallard who flew low over the fence and landed in the grass on the other side, instinctively faking a broken wing to draw the dog's attention to her and away from the ducklings. Though Zainy couldn't follow, the momentary distraction gave me time to grab her collar before she turned back to the ducklings. I plopped on my rump, the only way I could hold her back until my commands could bypass her own instincts.

I crated her again, glad to have avoided further Mallard massacre. When I went out to pick up the feathers I found one duckling, the ridged accordion of its neck so impossibly elongated that I thought its entire backbone had come loose. That one quick snap of Zainy's head. It hadn't had a chance.

Never before had I seen an example of 'bird brain' in action. Yet Ms. Mallard was back the next day with five ducklings. We called a company that removes ducks. My neighbor came over to say his wife was upset that I was taking them away. "They're awfully cute."

"Zainy *killed* one."

"Oh, I'm sure she didn't mean it," he said. "She probably thought it was a toy."

I shook my head. "She's a *dog*."

Despite the reality check I had for my neighbor, that night I tossed in bed, my sentence playing over and over in my head. "Zainy *killed* one." Yet Zainy herself was done with the incident. Because a dog doesn't spill regret throughout the house, doesn't lurk in a life of guilt and second-guessing.

It took me a few weeks to accept—on what now had to be a personal level—that nature is incidentally unkind, even when its face is that of a beloved pet. Yet Zainy remained thoughtlessly ecstatic, as if all of life's treats had been conjured just for her pleasure. When my kids grew into teenagers and couldn't be bothered to play in the pool, she remained the belly-flop queen, leaping after her water toys. When I swam, she matched me lap for lap. Into old age, she'd glide into the pool each night before coming into the house to sleep in her crate, more comfortable in an enclosed space. As I rubbed her down with towels, I wondered why she consistently launched herself into the water so late. And it came to me: she was getting a massage every night. She knew how to enjoy her life, moment to moment.

Fletcher and Zainy were always alert to their environment and the creatures in it. Because the wilderness park was in the foothills behind our neighborhood, wild creatures would sometimes make their way into our yard. Deer were the most common. I imagine other areas of the country consider this routine, but in crowded and hot suburbs, nature in the yard—even the presence of songbirds—is rare. The dogs were always on the opposite side of a fence from the guests, in the dog run or hanging out on the patio near the pool. If they remained quiet, displaying what appeared to be awe, the deer stayed, munching on the leaves of overgrown bushes. If the dogs got up to barking, the deer fled. These days, deer don't appear. Perhaps persistent drought has driven them off. Through the whole of the pandemic, I only witnessed them on rare occasions, on the edges of the wilderness park.

The bears disappeared from sight even before the pandemic, though they appear to lurk in the neighborhood each night before trash day, and our neighbors catch their images on house surveillance cameras. In Zainy and Fletcher's middle years, the bears were a regular source of daytime visitations. The dogs would rush the fence, mad with the desire to chase them, barking to wake the dead. Sometimes the bears lit out; sometimes they sauntered. Periodically, they would have a seat in the dry grasses, seeming to enjoy teasing the dogs. Once the dogs caught sight of a black bear and rushed the fence. The bear scurried up a pine tree and clung to it until, perhaps, it occurred to her that these were just dogs after all, and she was quite a bit more. She climbed down and slowpoked her way across the slope into the next yard, there being no fence at that height. There she plopped in front of a calf-high block wall that separated the manicured section of the neighbor's yard from their unkempt slope. She put her arms on the wall and set her chin on her hands as if she were some dreamy young girl contemplating her future. The dogs were hysterical, leaping and nearly achieving backflips in their desire to get to her.

My neighbors were kind but exacting people. Knowing this, I was worried when the husband approached us the day after the bear hysteria. When Fletcher was just a puppy, the neighbor had written a note complaining of his daytime barking. Not rudely or in a way that generated animosity between us. I answered that we'd gotten Fletcher as a rescue who wanted to be on the move, and he was letting everyone know, but that we were working with him and hoped they could be patient. Yes, they said, in that case, they could.

So, though it was years later, I was surprised when the neighbor said he was glad the dogs carried on so about the bear, alerting them to the fact it was in their yard. They might have walked out and startled it, and then what would have happened? Further, he wondered if we could leave the dogs out in the dog run at night, where they would be safe but could sound the alarm for each intruding bear.

No, I said, that wouldn't work. Honestly, I had a belief that dogs who stayed indoors at night lived longer, healthier lives. But without going into that reasoning, I pointed out that Fletcher and Zainy were likely to bark at anything in the night including skunks (who might then spray them), raccoons, and coyotes. Plus, other neighbors might not want to hear the alarm raised, but would prefer to sleep through bears knocking over their trashcans. At any rate, these elderly next-door neighbors might not have awakened no matter how the dogs carried on. During the Grand Prix Fire, when the neighborhood was surrounded in walls of flame and a truck drove through at midnight repeatedly blasting a horn and announcing over a loudspeaker that immediate evacuation was mandatory, they slept. This seemed impossible, and not seeing them, I assumed they had fled. But when David rang their doorbell and finally repeatedly slammed the side of his fist against their bedroom window as our sons and I were getting Fletcher settled into the back of the minivan, the wife, seeing him, called out, "David? Is there something wrong?"

Both our houses survived that fire, but areas of our yards were burned. The taller trees were not consumed, but the fire was the eventual death of them. One pine lasted several years in a half-burnt state of health. It was the tree the bear climbed that day. Like the dogs, it is no longer with us.

Of all Fletcher and Zainy's run-ins with nature (eventually, they were sprayed by a skunk—Zainy's fault I assumed, since she got the worst of it and was probably hoping to eat the creature), two incidents thrilled me with a sense of enchantment. The first happened when a coyote ventured into the yard, a now regular occurrence. Mostly they liked to tease the dogs, lying on the slope and watching them helplessly carry on. This one coyote came up to the wrought iron fencing around the patio and pool. He put his nose through the slats. From the other side, Fletcher and Zainy did the same. For a long moment they touched, a strange greeting. I wondered if this foreboded an illness in the coyote. Why would he do such a thing? But he looked very healthy in the way of wild animals living in the suburbs, those who feed on cats and the leftovers from garbage cans. The dogs' perfect stillness, their stance of attention, stretched necks, and raised coats were things I'd never seen. When I came close to the trio, the coyote fled.

On our regular hikes into the local hills, I sought emptiness and peace. Fletcher and Zainy found a thriving community of creatures, a heaven of scents to track, lizards and butterflies to snap at, and bugs to investigate. It was a virtual doggy activity center of the best sort. We never saw the mountain lions we were warned about in signage at all entrances. We did, however, see many deer, squirrels, and chipmunks on a regular basis, as well as the occasional skunk, rattlesnake, tarantula, and bobcat. The hills were also the home of the bears that entered our neighborhood, but they were more circumspect in midday, and sighting them was rare.

I liked always to have the dogs with me, partly because I would often come across single men in a lonely patch of the trail. I imagined each of these men was there for his own nature fix, but then, I was female and, alone, would have been easy prey. The two big dogs often caused men to take a wide path around me.

One day as we hiked an isolated trail away from the main loop, we turned a corner, coming around a vast toyon bush to stand face to face with a bear. I only had time to think *Oh shit!* before the bear turned and took off in the opposite direction. I would say bolted, but a big lumbering animal doesn't bolt, exactly. As it bounded away, the undulating edges of its black fur glistened in the sunlight, shedding quicksilver drops in its rays. I was trans-fixed. Even the dogs were silent and still, alert, a ridge of fur, head to tail, down each of their backs.

When the wilderness area was closed due to Santa Ana winds and the accompanying fire threat, the dogs demanded some sort of outdoor time and I'd often stay in the backyard with them for hours. Zainy would jump in the pool for a swim and come to shake right next to me, her favorite place to disperse water, sometimes nudging me from my reverie to get in the pool and play with her. During the summer and early fall, I'd swim or do stretching exercises. If she found I was too slow at tossing her toys, she would stand outside the pool, on the coping, a plastic squeaky ball full of water in her mouth. Coming close, she would squeeze it, a stream of water shooting from the squeaker onto my face. A friend suggested I get a video and win ten thousand dollars, but generally I was alone with the dogs.

During the relatively cooler seasons, I worked outside on my computer, read or listened to audiobooks. Over the years, I'd come to understand that by attending to the pups, I attended to myself in ways I wouldn't have otherwise. A red-tailed hawk would fly overhead, singular in the sky, which was bright blue, puffy-clouded, serene. The air was pleasant in fall and spring, hot for long summers, when the shade was often perfect. I looked up to see the tiny purple flowers of the lantana, the green hedge, the roses in bloom—pink, red, and sunset hues.

Enormous beauty surrounded me. All this felt like grace, and I was lucky each day I was with them.

For years we had this outdoor life, both Fletcher and Zainy continuing in good health beyond the average lifespan for dogs their size. The veterinarian had nicknamed Fletcher 'the Olympic athlete,' and I came to think of him this way. Why shouldn't he continue for decades with Zainy as his sidekick?

In all this time, Zainy followed Fletcher's lead, proving to be great outdoors. But she also loved the companionship of the family while Fletcher's interest in us remained connected to our willingness to be on the move with him.

Back when Zainy joined us, my second son, Patrick, was twelve. He's always been a constant reader. All during his high school, college, and grad school years, whenever he was home with us, he would walk around the yard or circle the pool, reading aloud. Zainy followed and listened, the best audience. She always loved the sound of voices, murmuring. Often before she fell asleep at night, she vocalized about her day, sounding much like the huskies I've seen in videos on social media. I don't think two dogs could have been more unalike in personalities, yet they became anxious when separated.

AGING

When he was fourteen, a lump started to form on Fletcher's upper right side, just behind his shoulder. Back in his day, Pongo had developed some lumps as he grew older. I'd never seen these on a dog and had them biopsied. They were just fatty deposits I was told, a natural part of aging. Having had this experience, I was less concerned about Fletcher's bump. But it grew in a way Pongo's never had. The vet biopsied it, pushed on it to get a sense of its density and declared it, too, a consequence of old age. Such tumors sometimes hardened, and had to be removed. The trouble was that Fletcher was already aged. Such a surgery could easily have been more dangerous to him than the lump itself, his survival not guaranteed.

About this time, a story was rolling through social media excoriating an owner who had left an old dog with a huge lump on its shoulder at a veterinary clinic. It occurred to me that the owner might not have had the money for an expensive operation that might not succeed and that this public shaming wasn't fair. It was also a lesson for me. I was afraid some nut bucket would see Fletcher's ever growing tumor, snap photos of our walks, and then proceed to shame me on social media for not caring for him, facts be damned. But I didn't want to leave Fletcher at home when his great joy in life was to be on the move outdoors. I hadn't thought of Fletcher as old because he was still so active. And the lump didn't harden, didn't get in his way, but it continued to expand. I made sure to always walk with Zainy on my right side, and

Fletcher on my left, his tumor next to my leg and far less visible to anyone passing us.

During this hide-the-tumor period, I read an article about how dogs can get liquid-based lumps, which were resolved through draining. Back to the vet we went. He explained while this tumor wasn't hard, it was a solid, not a liquid, and couldn't be drained. He again measured it, stretching the pincer-shaped tool to its limit. I was beginning to wonder if Fletcher would eventually fall over sideways if the lump expanded further.

Three months before his fifteenth birthday, Fletcher started showing other signs of his age. Still, he reminded me of the puppy we'd met at the shelter when he paced the wall, looking for an opening. When a new ailment appeared, he just tried a workaround.

Both dogs had an aversion to the blow dryer, Zainy defending herself against the attacking enemy by biting it. The easiest way to end a bath was to towel dry the pups and then give them each several chew treats as a reward for being good during the scrub down. A bonus to the routine was the entertainment it provided, keeping them from playing in the dirt, while they dried in the sun.

One afternoon as we sat in the sunshine, Fletcher looked perturbed. He'd finished his post-bath bully sticks and had moved on to a Nylabone chew. When I looked closely, I saw his gums were bleeding, so I took the stick away. He regularly chewed dental sticks and still had all his teeth, which looked like they were in fair shape. This was the first time I thought *Oh, he's too old for that*, something I repeated from that day forward. But Fletcher didn't think so. He pulled and strove to get at Zainy's treats until she finished them. Finally, he lay on the cozy round porch bed. I sat on the porch glider with the hope he'd stay settled, at least until he was dry. Stuck with no other entertainment, he gave in to something he usually couldn't be bothered with for long: he let me pet him as much as I liked.

Then came the day we headed out for a hike, but Fletcher was dragging his back legs as he walked. Thinking it would do more harm than good to continue, I decided to walk back and forth on a little cul-de-sac, not venturing more than a block from home while seeing if the leg trouble would work itself out. It didn't. I took Fletcher into the backyard to watch him move. He didn't seem to be in any pain, but then he had never whined about anything. I wondered if he'd had a mini stroke. I took him to the vet, who watched Fletcher pace.

Our veterinarian told me that Fletcher's back legs giving out were a sign of osteoarthritis, and a common one at that. He prescribed Rimadyl, saying it would help for a time. It did, and Fletcher could walk, but not uphill, putting his hikes as my companion to an end. Eventually, he began dragging his back feet again. Yet he had no patience for sitting around, and became anxious if I tried to walk Zainy without taking him along, at least part of the way. Finally his feet dragged to the point that he was scraping the top of his paws, leading to raw, bleeding patches. I found some dog shoes online. They were meant to give the wearer traction in the snow and ice, to keep feet warm. There's no such thing as a freeze in our neck of the woods, but the shoes had a hard plastic top covering the toes, much like the band of rubber on children's sneakers.

Lifting his legs in awkward poses as he attempted to walk with the shoes, Fletcher made us laugh. But when we were outside on the street, they did the job. He dragged and the plastic covering the toes took the scraping. He came back from his brief outings injury free. But he couldn't understand why he was returning so soon even though his hind quarters buckled in the effort to move. We'd reach our driveway, and Fletcher would turn back toward the street, nose thrust far forward, pulling with all his might in the effort to continue.

Perhaps, I told the veterinarian, Fletcher would like to be pulled in a wagon. The vet didn't think so. Fletcher wanted to walk where his senses were engaged. He would probably jump out of the wagon. How would I keep him in, me in my late fifties, continually picking up a good-sized dog? It was true. My back now screamed from bending over to bathe the dogs. We were all aging. I was just doing it a bit more slowly.

On these visits, I would tell the vet about Pongo, how he very suddenly dropped dead. At the time it was horrifying. Now, I was wondering if there had been a gift in it. "Fletcher will not drop dead," the vet told me. "He's the old athlete who will push and push himself, even though he's breaking down. You'll have to decide when it's time to say goodbye. But you'll know when to do that."

"How will I know?" I asked, more than once. I'd bring Fletcher in for a review of his health, fearing I would cause him undo suffering but not wanting to let him go, my much-loved companion through the thousands of running, hiking, and walking miles.

"When the bad times outweigh the good times," the vet said. "As long as he's engaged with you and his environment, and you don't mind taking care of him, his life has value." I began to weigh each moment and event, at first mentally, and later writing down at the end of each day whether it had been bad or good.

During all this Zainy continued hiking the hills with me. Until one day, when she was twelve and a half, she stopped on the trail. She was panting although the weather was mild enough. "Are you tired?" I asked her, offering water. She wasn't interested in drinking. Could she, that suddenly, be done with the hills? Curious, I stepped forward. She pulled back. Indeed, she was done. We turned toward home. She never wanted to hike again. Perhaps she was in pain although, like Fletcher, she didn't show it or complain. I let her make the call. Our days of the hills, with deer sightings, red tailed hawks and meadowlarks, bear spotting, and even lizard chasing, were over.

Fletcher declined. He would only eat dry food if it was mixed with so much canned food that it loosened his bowels. Though he still walked pretty well, he often had a hard time getting up from lying down. He began to shit on his cot and thus on himself, fairly regularly. The weather was warm, so we left him in the dog run at night with two cots. If he pooped on the first, he would get up and lie on the second. The cots were easier to clean than other options. I could disinfect them and pressure spray through the canvas-like material, which dried quickly.

I felt sorry for Fletcher having to have his rump cleaned regularly because he still hated water. He wasn't long for this world, but he was still engaged, doing the things the vet had noted as part of a good life. While in the yard, he'd sniff around. Since his walks had stopped, he began coming up to me in regular intervals to be petted and loved, a change I welcomed.

I didn't think he would last until the weather got cold. What would I do if he was still having more good than bad times? Would it be okay to leave him in the dog run with his cots if it was, say, fifty degrees out at night? What if it got closer to forty degrees? I couldn't crate him as he would be lying in his own excrement. I couldn't have him pooping in the house every night and dragging crap as he got up. The decision was harder than the vet made it sound.

While Fletcher's back legs continued to weaken, he got around, engaged with family and entertained by Zainy. The last thing I wanted to do was euthanize him too soon as if he were a nuisance. I'd had three kids, changed thousands of diapers and was at the beginning of my journey with an incontinent parent. The clean up wasn't a deciding factor for someone so used to it. I wanted to stick with 'more bad days than good days' as my decision criteria. I made two fleece sweaters with Velcro closures, easy to put on and take off. I created a little 'igloo' area, enclosed in blankets, at the inside corner of the patio, up against the house, out of the wind, where the heat radiated from the plaster walls.

MORTALITY

At night, I had to keep Zainy away from Fletcher or she would pull his sweaters off. Other than that, I was happy with my arrangement. Each morning, I got up early to check on Fletcher. He was usually asleep, and I'd place my hand on his side, pet him over the sweater, chat a bit until he was fully awake. The air around him was warm. He was warm. This is okay, I'd think. More good than bad.

Fletcher had trouble getting off the cot, but I could tilt him toward the ground, and he'd find his feet. Once he was up and started to move, I had the sense that his bones warmed, his stiffness left. Couldn't we make it through winter this way? Why shouldn't Fletcher see his sixteenth birthday in April?

When I woke him in the morning, he was excited and paced back and forth, action that spoke to me of an energy reserve tapped through medication. Yet, when we attempted our walks to the end of the cul-de-sac, which would best be measured in feet rather than fractions of a mile, Fletcher's legs collapsed under him. I would wait, let the moment pass, and then continue home. By January, we had to stop because it looked like he was afraid. Now, he didn't pull back toward the street demanding to move. We could hang around the house, then, enjoying each other's company. More good than bad.

At the end of January, I woke early and made my way outside to help Fletcher up from his cot. I saw him, not in his cozy corner blanket tent, but lying awake on the cold cement of the patio. Had he felt the urge to relieve himself, a thing he usually slept through? Why had he gotten up before I could help him? *Oh god*, I thought. *I did this. My fault. My fault.* I tried to pull him up, but his legs were unsteady.

He couldn't get purchase on the completely smooth concrete. His front legs splayed like Bambi's, and, of course, his back legs were so weak.

I held him around his belly until he was stable enough to move on his own. While I wrapped myself around him, Fletcher's back was pressed into my chest. I could feel the knuckles of his spine, evidence that what I'd been imagining as a sudden weight loss was a certain reality.

More bad than good.

Now I was afraid I wouldn't be able to turn away from the 'next-level' care I had been administering. I wanted to keep coming up with solutions to Fletcher's demise, but the truth was obvious: he was suddenly and rapidly declining. Lifting him elicited that strange 'smile' that dogs in pain sometimes fool their humans with.

Patrick wished we could release Fletcher into the wilderness to venture outward, as he loved to do, until he fell into a permanent sleep. A thought full of romance, but we lived in the real world. If Fletcher were euthanized in the wilderness where he'd once spent the night alone as a juvenile, the outcome might have involved a pack of coyotes or a mountain lion.

The way I would get through euthanizing him was to schedule it as if it were an ordinary veterinarian appointment, giving myself more than a week to get used to the idea. The vet tried to give me some assurance with the story of a Buddhist family he knew who didn't believe in ending any life. He understood their commitment, but detailed how horribly and, he felt, unnecessarily, their dog had suffered in his last days.

I decided on a Thursday appointment because Alejandro had no college classes that day and could drive the two hours from San Diego for a long weekend. He wanted to say goodbye. Though I'd at first hoped the vet would come to the house, David was opposed to it. I realized there was an underlying aspect to his reasoning, and as I thought about it, I agreed. His mother, who was ninety-three at the time, lived with us. What would it be like to be certain that one's own death was near—she died at ninety-five—and watch this procedure?

Planning ahead and paying ahead meant that every day I thought: how strange that Fletcher won't be here.

In three days,

in two days,

in twenty-four hours,

I'm not going to have my good old boy.

On each of these mornings I would think, *Well, he's getting up okay. Maybe I should cancel.* Thursday morning as I held him to clean him off, his pain was evident. His appointment wasn't until two PM because I'd imagined Alejandro coming from San Diego that morning and running into traffic. Nervous and grieving, he'd arrived Wednesday night. All Thursday morning, I sat with Fletcher, waiting, an internal timer racing through the seconds. On the short trip to the vet, he pooped in the car, seeming to have lost his ability to control his bowels.

When we arrived, the vet assured us that Fletcher had greatly deteriorated since he'd last seen him. Before, even though Fletcher was old and losing muscle mass and having a hard time with his back legs, he was curiously snooping around the exam room, eager for the treats the vet always dispensed at the end of a visit. Now he simply reclined on the scale next to me. He weighed only fifty pounds, quite a drop from his high of sixty-two. The bumps along his spine pressed into my hand as I petted him.

The vet explained to the family what he had gone over with me more than once, those times I had brought Fletcher in wondering how his life would end. He was about to receive fifty times the amount of anesthetic used for surgery. His pain center would shut down immediately. He would pass within thirty minutes, but might have a muscle spasm. I remembered Pongo's sudden convulsing at death and worried about this. But no.

Fletcher was silent and still, gone within a minute. So quickly, it was hard to believe. A friend later told me the rapidity with which a dog passes while being euthanized indicates how close it already is to death. I don't know if this is true, but it made me sad, thinking again, that I hadn't judged correctly, had waited too long.

This death was another reminder of the terrible time I had letting go of anyone who mattered to me.

Alejandro was also badly broken up, but I was glad he was there to see how quickly and painlessly Fletcher's life could end.

My other sons were busy with their lives. Matthew was at work in San Diego. Patrick was in Chicago in his PhD program. When we Skyped with him, Patrick told us he'd had two dreams about

Fletcher. First he dreamed that Fletcher was, in a very anthropo-morphic way, using a shovel to dig up things in the backyard. They were just things the Fletcher of the dream thought were cool, but had no intrinsic value. Two nights later, he dreamed he saw Fletcher and wondered that he hadn't been put down. I told him we'd taken Fletcher, but it didn't work so we brought him home. When we next saw Matthew, he said he'd had a similar dream about Fletcher—that we brought him home because the euthanasia didn't work.

The discussion of dreams bothered me. I had no dreams about Fletcher. I thought back to when Pongo died and my dreams of apologizing to him for not walking him enough, for not creating his best life during the time I was so overwhelmed. But with Fletcher, I was always present. Perhaps there was nothing I was trying to work out, no dream contrition. Yet, it would have been nice to have a dream of him running in the hills.

The Wednesday following Fletcher's death, Zainy got up in the morning only to have her back legs repeatedly collapse under her. She wasn't dragging them the way Fletcher had done. Instead, she looked uncoordinated, as if she didn't understand the concept of walking. They would slide from under her. That went on through-out the day. She seemed dazed, out of it, unable to focus on me or anything I said to her.

She was two and a half years younger than Fletcher. Was she too going to die, and in the same week? Whereas Fletcher's demise had been slow, it seemed that Zainy was repeating it all in a day. I didn't want to believe this was happening.

Thursday morning we took her to the vet. "Did she have a

stroke?" I asked.

No, the vet told me, it was the weakening of the muscles in the back legs. Her hips were certainly hurting.

"Why would it happen overnight?"

"Sometimes that happens with dogs who are engaged and interested in life," he told me. "They put up with pain until it overcomes them."

I thought *Is this what dog grief looks like?* Without Fletcher to mimic, without her lifelong playmate and hiking partner, perhaps her pain became foremost.

After an exam and some blood work, the vet prescribed Galliprant for the arthritic aches. Although our dogs had never needed to have their nails clipped—they wore down in the many miles of walking and jogging each week—Zainy's nails were now growing unevenly, apparently because she was putting pressure on her front legs to walk, favoring her weakened back legs. I had her nails clipped before we went home.

Zainy's medication changed her outlook overnight. She engaged with me, her legs regained their coordination, and the slipping stopped. We returned to the vet for a checkup. I was very excited about Zainy's renewal and reminded him that Fletcher had made it to almost sixteen. He said, "Victoria, not everyone is an Olympic athlete," a gentle reminder that Zainy was herself already thirteen. She was not Fletch the Olympian.

Despite her renewed interest in the world around her, Zainy showed signs of missing Fletcher. Her dog grief mostly took the form of finding things with Fletcher's scent and puzzling out why they didn't lead to him. I hadn't had the heart to do anything with the fleece wrap-arounds I'd made him. Zainy found them. She buried her nose in them, pushing the fabric. She dug at them with her claws and then flipped them into the air. But there was no abracadabra moment. Fletcher did not appear from under the pile.

David and I brought dinner to my parents every Sunday, cajoling David's mother into coming with us because we didn't want to leave her in the house alone. She was always bored during these visits since my mom, suffering from dementia, was unable to carry on a conversation and continually repeated herself, forgetting what was said only minutes before. The dynamic often filled me with anxiety, but after Fletcher's death and the scare with Zainy, I felt especially gloomy.

While we were going through the drama of caring for ailing dogs, our own parents required increasing levels of care. We'd helped my parents move into a gated senior community because their large house and yard were too much to handle, even with outside help. My mother had part-time caregiving. My dad had pre-leukemia and severe anemia, conditions that left him breathless and chronically tired. His 'condolence' in this, if you could call it that, was his doctor's assurance that he would die of old age before he had full-blown leukemia.

I had few topics of conversation to engage my parents. We were on opposite ends of the political and social spectrum, and I wasn't much for arguing, especially with a man who was largely deaf, hearing only when shouted at.

On the Sunday after Zainy's scare, we arrived to my dad

announcing that he hadn't had any ice cream as an afternoon snack because he wanted to eat the big dinner he knew he'd have. This was a compliment to David, who'd cooked. As we ate, I filled my parents in on Fletcher's travails, which were followed by Zainy's. My dad said, "That's what it is to get old." A terrible sense came over me. I'd known how to get Fletcher through the end, to mitigate his suffering, while keeping him with us as long as possible. I had no idea how to do that for my parents.

Neither of my parents told many stories about their youths. But the talk of dogs drew my dad in. He told a story of his boyhood. His grandmother had come to stay with his family and brought her dog along. Perhaps she was recovering from an illness, but the story wasn't centered on her. Her dog took a shine to my dad, a boy of twelve or so. "And that dog was smart, too," my dad said. Every day it waited for him after school at the bus stop. They were fast friends.

When the time came for his grandmother to go back to her own home, my dad cried inconsolably. "Don't worry, you'll see Grandma again," his parents told him. But the unspeakable truth was he cried for the loss of his buddy, the mutt.

How comforting that his memory of the long ago friendship with his grandmother's dog reminded us of something important we had in common.

I took a ten-day trip to New York and then on to Ireland with my sisters. When I came back, it was easier to see how Zainy was aging. She walked like someone with creaking bones and barked with her old gal voice, sounding like a seal. When we went out in the morning, she trotted past the pool over to the gate leading toward the dog run. Seeing her stand there, I might have thought she was getting a bit senile; instead, I wondered if she thought Fletcher was out there, where he would have been in the morning, separated from her during breakfast, since she'd eat all his food otherwise. She was seeking her buddy. After a few weeks, she stopped waiting.

About this time, we had a leak under the bathroom floor and knew we needed some major repairs. As our decor was stuck in the 1970s—the kitchen had a drop ceiling to accommodate long bars of fluorescent lights—we decided we would have our home remodeled, a months-long project. While touring the house, the architect stopped in the hallway next to a photo of Fletcher. "That's a beautiful dog," he said.

"He was," I answered.

Not wanting to pack and unpack what was no longer needed, I began clearing out storage spaces and closets throughout the house.

Our laundry room storage held everything belonging to the dogs. In a bin under the dryer, I found old ear rinse, eye rinse, Flys Off, training collars, a long training leash, two short leashes with reflective tape for our many after-work walks in the dark night, and dog collars that Zainy had outgrown long ago. Toss, toss, toss.

And then there was Fletcher's collar, larger, heavier, with a good metal clasp, and so worn I knew it was red only by memory. Well past use for another dog. Smooth along its surface was the metal dog tag that helped return him to us more than once. It never came off. The one he wore when he ambled up to the old folks in a beautiful assisted living center established in an old house of round granite stones.

The nametag had FLETCHER written in bold uppercase, followed by lines with my name, my phone number, my address.

Before tossing the old collar in the trash, I slid the nametag out. I know I won't have another dog named Fletcher—the tag is useless now, its service done. The previous day, Facebook automatically served up an old photo of him as a memory. He was much older in that image than in his escape artist days, but much younger than when he was ill. He was still, looking eager to get going. He was in that perfect state of being my companion, still fully capable of speeding through hills, yet, graciously, willing to move through the world with me in tow.

AGING

I've never been good at knowing when to give up, a personality trait that has harmed me in bad friendships and romances. But it has an upside when I serve another who is genuinely in need. While relationships with dogs, unlike those with people, are free of subterfuge and manipulation, that I had end-of-life decisions entirely in my hands was another sort of complication bringing stress. I alternately chided myself for quitting too soon with Fletcher and for causing him to suffer by failing to recognize when the bad outweighed the good.

I began comparing Zainy's old age to Fletcher's, hoping to do what was best for her. Just like Fletcher, she had no comprehension of what she was no longer able to do. But whereas an anthropomorphic Fletcher might have been summarized with Dylan Thomas's "Do not go gentle into that good night"—"Rage, rage, against the dying of the light"—when Zainy failed at something, she knew not to try it again. If she were a person, she might have memorized the lyrics to "Don't Worry, Be Happy."

One day, I sat with Patrick by the fountain in our yard. Zainy was with us and decided to go up the steep slope behind the fountain. She got caught up in the vines of the neighbor's ground cover. My own age a deterrent, I couldn't get purchase at that angle. Patrick stepped up to help her when she turned around to come back, stumbling and rolling. I thought she might roll all the way down into the neighbor's yard and really hurt herself, but her weight held her in place after a few yards. It was clear she was frightened and unsure of how she'd collapsed. She never tried to wander on the slope again.

We continued with brief walks on flat ground. She would make for dry leaves and crunch them to her heart's delight. I was glad to have the chance to be out with her, often at sunset when the neighborhood had cooled down. We'd walk east for a half-mile and then turn west to head home. The sky was gray and pink, the horizon gold. If clouds appeared, they were flat on the bottom but thick and puffy above. I would have missed so much of the beauty surrounding me if I hadn't taken seriously my duty to the dogs.

Zainy's legs again started to slip out from under her. I hoped the vet could increase her medication as it had been so beneficial for over a year. He said it didn't work that way. It was time to keep a journal, note any difficulties or evident pain, and assess each day as good or bad.

Though my mother-in-law spent the four seasons of the year alternating living with her four children, she still owned her home in the city adjacent to ours. We moved into her house while the remodel was underway. She would live with us there when she returned from Seattle, a few days after we got situated. She didn't like dogs inside the house, had never allowed any of her own to be. I couldn't have Zainy outside at night, afraid that her legs would collapse under her, and no one would come to her aid. Zainy still had control of her bowels during the night, so she could sleep in a crate, something she'd always liked, I believe, because she was naturally anxious and felt covered and safe. Just in front of the door leading to the backyard, there was a small patch of linoleum in an otherwise carpeted room. My mother-in-law agreed that we could place the crate on the linoleum and have Zainy sleep there, just inside the door.

We'd only had this arrangement a few days, when David's mom returned from Seattle. She was tired from her journey and slept early that night, only to awaken in the morning saying she had such trouble breathing, she felt like she was dying. We called 9-1-1, and David followed the ambulance to the hospital. Esther had pneumonia, not for the first time in her old age. But the strongest antibiotics made no progress against it. She was diagnosed with congestive heart failure and couldn't keep up with the liquid filling her lungs. She had been right when she said she was dying. At ninety-five, she had lived a full life, and appeared unafraid of death, a thing I'd never before witnessed. A thing I aspire to, but don't yet see myself achieving.

Esther was moved to a long-term hospital specializing in respiratory care. Greeting her many relatives who lived in the area and visited frequently, she sometimes complained that death was taking too long and she was bored of lying around, but otherwise remained stolid.

During our first days of shuttling back and forth to the hospital, Zainy developed a terrible bout of diarrhea; at the same time her right front leg was slipping out from under her. David would stare at her as she slowly toured the backyard. "You have to put that dog down, you can't let her suffer like that," he'd say. I went back to the trusted vet.

The veterinarian thought Zainy had probably eaten a toxic insect and also hyperextended her leg due to the stress of holding herself on front legs more since her back legs were so weak. It was just a coincidence that the two happened at the same time. After resting the hyperextended leg and taking a course of antibiotics as well as a probiotic to reset her gut, Zainy was pretty good. Of course, she was old and stiff, but no longer limping. We tried some new foods she liked, and her bowels stabilized. Later, as Patrick (again visiting from Chicago) and I took walks together, he mentioned David was projecting his experience with his mom, who was so close to dying—a situation over which he had no control—to Zainy, a loved one for whom he might prevent suffering.

Esther died while we were staying at her house. Her belief in a Catholic heaven—that is in the community of saints, which she would join and which included her husband, who had died seven years earlier—was certain. I had been raised in the same church, which also taught that pets didn't make it to the afterlife, but could be blessed by the priest for a long life. I had walked away from the church some years before, when its handling of the clergy's sexual abuse cases became known. I don't have the certainty in the afterlife that my mother-in-law had, but whenever I imagine myself as a soul in a next world, I can't see it without dogs.

Knowing that Zainy's life would come to a close within the year, our nuclear family gatherings—all three adult sons over for dinner—would sometimes turn to discussions of what that meant. Maybe there was a rainbow bridge. "She'd sprint directly for Fletcher."

"I don't think she'll ever catch up with Fletcher. He would have started running in a straight line and never stopped."

If the afterlife was going to be a pleasure for people or for dogs, it would have to be outside of space and time.

Zainy was experiencing several bouts of anxiety over common, everyday events. Since she didn't like being groomed by strangers, we gave her baths in the backyard when she was young. I got older and my back bothered me more at the same time Zainy was less mobile. We started taking her to doggy wash shops where the tub was at chest level. Her last doggy wash was a disaster. She hadn't been in the car in a few months. She wasn't able to step up inside. We couldn't lift her without causing distress, so we had to get her into a crate, then pick up the crate and slide it into the back of Alejandro's car. When we arrived, we had to lower the crate to the ground. Once in the shop, she had a hard time walking up the steps to the bath. Although she had been through this process many times and generally loved water, she started shaking, seeming scared. I gave her a quick wash with some gentle talk. We still had never used a blow dryer on her, and so toweled her off. As we walked her out of the shop, she pooped on the floor. That was not so bad though I figured she was certainly stressed. I had some doggie bags with me, and went to clean it up. Alejandro said, "You missed a little." I gave him the second bag to get that tiny spot and while we were doing that, Zainy moved forward and took a big, wet dump on the floor and then fell down into it, likely because her old legs had been standing too long. I was out of bags, so I had to kind of turn that second bag inside out, and use what I could.

I told an employee that I had this problem. She went to the back and got some disinfectant and paper towels. Thankfully, I had some medical latex gloves, and I used those, but it took forever, was the biggest mess. While I was cleaning up, Alejandro took

Zainy outside. He happened to have some old towels in his car. He used a hand towel to wash her backside and then threw it in the trash. When we got home, I had to wash Zainy's backside again, starting over. I lifted her, and my back responded, pulsing electric waves of pain.

I thought of my mother, her dementia causing her to regress. My sisters and I were partly responsible for her care. She would become nearly hysterical when we tried to help with her personal hygiene. She would scream at us, "No! Goddammit, I said no!" Her mid-twentieth century Catholic loathing of the body and its functions were amplifying the daily nightmare of caretaking. It was unnerving, and her doctor prescribed the anti-anxiety medication Ativan, to see if we could get her to cooperate.

With dogs, caretaking was so much simpler. Zainy didn't have to have any more baths. Despite the disaster of her doggy wash trip, she immediately relaxed when she was home. She could still swim, and if she continued to do so when the weather warmed she would be okay. In the meantime, it was to her I went to tell my woes of parental caretaking. I had started this a decade earlier when my mom's dementia became evident. Later, I continued by whispering the challenges of having a mother-in-law in my house. Finally, I lamented the heightened difficulty of caring for both my parents as their health failed, and my father had more than one near-death emergency. Perhaps Patrick's having read to her all her life conditioned Zainy to be a dog who liked to listen to the lilt of human voices. Her sitting with me as I murmured throughout the morning hours was a blessing.

MORTALITY

I began to dream about Zainy regularly, each night's reel emblematic of daylight's realities. Soon after our doggy wash debacle, I had a two-part dream. As it began, I was on a trip with my family. People I knew from various walks of my life were there. We were all looking for the best things to do on our journey, figuring out how to get to the desirable sites. Without warning the atmosphere flipped, and I found myself near a shaft that reminded me of a laundry chute, except it descended at a 45-degree angle rather than being vertical. Zainy had fallen into it. David and I were trying to figure out how to get her back. She was clawing upward but never getting to the top. I jumped up to run down some stairs, hoping to figure out if there was an opening on the bottom where I could release her. Just then, she clawed up a bit, and I was able to grab her and pull her out.

The scene changed, and I was outside with her. She was on a leash, and we walked a little bit. I thought, 'Oh, I need a bag in case she has to poop. I reached in my sweatshirt pocket and felt a plastic bag, so I pulled it out. It was already full of poop, thick and tightly tied at the top. I thought I had something to cover an emergency and then realized I had used up all my emergency supplies.

These thoughts about Zainy made sense. In reality, she began having a terrible time with her back legs, often falling to a sitting position and not being able to get up. I would pull her up from behind. Truly, I had no emergency supplies left—her medication wasn't working very well anymore; she was very far gone. She began to poop and pee on her outdoor bed because it was the softest, easiest place to go. Even when she made an effort, she regularly pooped on the porch, unable to get to an appropriate spot fast enough.

No tricks left up my sleeve. Nothing hidden in my pockets. More bad than good. I scheduled our last appointment with the vet.

It was February 2020, and we were a few weeks from our initial pandemic lockdown. My favorite aunt—who had once saved me from drowning in a pool—had just passed away. My father, in addition to the severe anemia, now had episodes of internal bleeding, and was actively dying. My sisters and I alternated spending nights with him and our mom, whose dementia prevented her from having a clear idea of what was happening, of why we were living with her, and at times, even who we were. I would have given a good deal to have Zainy with me a little longer, knowing my parents would soon be gone. But life doesn't create separate and distinct grief boxes that we can move into place. Instead, grief was layered, suffocatingly thick.

Zainy's passing was as quick as Fletcher's, as painless, and even more heartbreaking. I wrote her a short eulogy, hoping to understand something of the numerous endings I was coming to, to acknowledge that I had always felt some part of Fletcher remained with us while she was here. Now they were both truly gone.

Together we'd jogged, hiked, trained for marathons, and walked—literally—thousands of miles. My constant outdoor companions, they pulled me through the crisis that midlife is. They got me outdoors, and I had the perks of seeing and hearing the birds while nature bloomed around me. Patrick made up funny nicknames for them all the time. Our favorite was *salchicha* (sausage) for Zainy. Alejandro grew up with them. Now we faced the impending death of both my parents without our pups just as a pandemic emerged.

LIFE/TRANSIENCE

For weeks after Zainy died, I compulsively looked at photos of her on my iPad, shedding silent tears. One of the last was of her standing just outside the sliding glass door on an early morning. She had been barking at me, refusing to come in, demanding instead that I come out so she wouldn't be alone. In the photo she looked ancient—her posture squat, her back legs bent, not only her face, but all the fur over her head pure white. Her eyes were cloudy. Yet when I acquiesced and sat on the porch glider to pet her, she was alert on her bed, her profile showing the perfect shape of her head, her nose lifted to the atmosphere. My outdoor girl to the end. And this is how I continue to see her in memory, a being attuned to life.

Shortly after Zainy passed, the pandemic blasted into our lives. My sisters and I were temporarily barred from caring for our parents as their assisted living apartments went into full lockdown. We circumvented the rules by registering with the facility as self-employed caretakers.

This caretaking environment was especially depressing, as everything in the apartments was closed—no bingo games, not even a dining room. Tepid meals were delivered in cardboard cartons. My parents didn't have outdoor space. Neither of them was mobile. I felt stuck in a madhouse, my father in hallucinatory pain as death closed in, my mother unable to understand reality but feeling some primordial and deep-seated fear that manifested in inappropriate outbursts. In a repeating six-day cycle, I was locked in the tiny apartment for three days and two nights.

When I'd come home for the three days of the six, I had no pup to soothe my weary soul. David was sympathetic and always helpful, but he had his own griefs. How much easier it had been to unburden myself to Zainy, whose presence alone was soothing. When my dad died at the end of April, my mom couldn't remember where he went and asked about his whereabouts repeatedly. By then, the pandemic was raging. With no clear federal plan for eradication, my sisters and I knew our isolation and difficulties would be long-term. We arranged to move our mom to a rented house so we could both visit and caretake as we chose. We hired more help as it took two people to lift, toilet, and bathe mom. We would stay only Fridays through Mondays—the full time caretaker's days off, lessening our contact with others. Nevertheless, I once had to have a COVID test after being in contact with outside caretakers and becoming ill (happily, it was negative). Later, I was required to quarantine for ten days after a visiting nurse, who had no symptoms, tested positive a few days after having a conversation with me about my mom's lack of mobility.

I'd originally thought waiting out the pandemic without dogs was a good idea—I was so often gone from home to fulfill my caretaking duties, and though David liked dogs, he wasn't loopy over them the way I was. Yet, without a dog, I was faltering. My emotional state became my environment. Like a woman in tropical humidity, my sorrow was a layer of sweat. It was the vapor surrounding me; I exhaled it and then breathed it back in, never escaping. Often, in free moments as my mom napped, I perused animal shelter websites, imagining various dogs coming home with me. Each dog that would make an appropriate placement was snatched up immediately. Clearly, in the heart of a pandemic, I was among many who felt alone and needed a companion. A close friend of mine who knew how badly I was faltering recommended a dog rescue in San Diego, one where a friend of hers often delivered homeless dogs found on the streets of Tijuana.

One day as I perused the rescue website, I saw that a nursing mom and her four pups had been brought up from Mexico. She appeared to be a Border collie mix, longhaired, black and tan. One of her pups looked like her, but in puppy version, this was a sort of cuddly little bear, a furry puff with big black eyes. He was immediately spoken for. The other pups looked nothing like mom. One, a shorthaired chestnut had several irregular patches of white—boots, a zagging necklace, and off center white stripe up his snout. His eyes were the same chestnut as his fur but the black edges of his eyelids emphasized their beauty. He looked like he'd grow up to be a good sixty pounds. I put in a request and filled out all the forms indicating that I was emotionally and financially capable of caring for him. On July 11, 2020, David and I drove the one hundred and twenty miles to pick him up.

When we arrived, the puppy charmed us. He playfully wrestled stuffed toys and would wander over to his mom, who clearly was done with him. The rescuers laughed and said mom was available as well. But between dogs and family members, I'd experienced several deaths in the last three years and laid my bets on youth. Another puppy from the same litter looked just like 'Clove' except that she was all white with barely distinguishable tan markings over her ears and eyes. The rescuer said, "Salt is available, too. The adopters came all the way from Ventura yesterday to pick her up, but they didn't feel a connection."

We looked at the adorable pup. Someone came two hundred miles to take her home and then left without her. Why?

David and I huddled. We wanted two dogs because a single would be too lonely. Our plan had been to purchase a Labrador retriever after several months, primarily because we'd loved Zainy so much and thought the breed had been part of that. What if we just took both dogs with us? One of the rescuers said she'd always heard it wasn't good to have two dogs from the same litter although she didn't know from where that wisdom derived. The other thought it would be fun. As the two pups played together, we could see they'd bonded. Why not?

As Matthew and Alejandro lived in San Diego, we stopped by to show them the pups and order a meal. We'd already picked the name Loki for the chestnut pup. Now, with the two dogs, we wondered if we should try something cute instead like 'Whiskey' and 'Soda,' but we're not big drinkers. Watching Salt exploring the small patio and yard of the condominium, pulling at the foliage and trying to squeeze through the boards of the fence, we came up with her name—Curiosa, a nod to her behavior as well as to Furiosa from *Mad Max: Fury Road*.

Two eight-week old puppies were a brand new reminder of my age. Although they had wonderful round bellies, they somehow managed to squeeze between the rails of the wrought-iron fence. We'd ordered fencing for a new dog run, complete with a roof (still fearing those coyotes) but it hadn't yet arrived. We added a mesh tarp along the fence around the yard, but the dogs still had to be watched all the time they were outside. They loved to eat the bark in the mulch, munch on plants and generally try out anything that could make them sick. I'd fetch one and the other would get into mischief.

The patch over Curiosa's eye and ear darkened, and I nicknamed her RCA, after the pup who listened to a record on the RCA label. (This didn't stick. We've since come up with multiple nicknames.) Now Curiosa has dark tan patches, spots in various places and black freckles all through her skin. Loki's coloring remains the same with the addition of some freckles along his snout. In their relationship, it's clear Curiosa is dominant. She hogs toys and regularly leads whatever activity they devise. She's bright and has made up several weird games, shredding three cots in order to use them as places to drop a ball through a hole and then try to find it by jumping on the cot and forcing the ball to roll out in the open. It's a doggie version of whack-a-mole.

We had a harder than usual time with puppy escapades. I thought back to the admonition not to have littermates together. The dogs chewed one another's collars off multiple times until, exasperated, we bought chain collars, which are not nearly as cute. If one pup reacts to a new stimulus, the other joins in solidarity. Early on, walks were a nightmare when other dogs appeared on the path. Less crazy but still trouble were scooters, bikes, strollers, joggers, and skateboards. If a lizard or squirrel crossed the path, I braced for the bolt. It was impossible for me to take both dogs out. David came with me or I took the dogs separately. When I did, Curiosa would whine until Loki returned. Although she didn't mind walking without him, she couldn't stand to be left behind.

The trainer, to whom we ventured weekly, encouraged us, saying persistence would pay off. She was right. Coming into constant contact with the variety of life outdoors has helped to settle both dogs. Loki, who was anxious, is now full of joy on his ventures, always eager to say hello to a horse who lives on the other side of the fence along our path.

We've bought 'indestructible' cots and beds. We've been through a variety of foods, finding what works for their sensitive stomachs and skin. Fearing a lack of socialization during the pandemic, we regularly took them to doggy daycare until they both came home with a case of kennel cough although they'd had the bordetella vaccine. After seeing rattlesnakes hugging the edge of our house twice within two weeks, we had the pups vaccinated against rattlesnake bites. They're microchipped, a thing that would have proven invaluable twenty years ago with Fletcher.

David has joked that with all the expensive foods, destroyed dog toys and equipment, and torn up landscape, we wouldn't have been able to afford these dogs when we were younger. There's some truth to this. And while all this could be frustrating, puppy escapades and the stress they induced never felt like the anxiety train other parts of my pandemic life had been. In life's notebook, puppies are a lot more good than bad.

So we are making our way. Sixty-five and sixty pounds respectively, Loki and Curiosa have grown into the dogs I imagined. They look like hunting hounds—think of a Dalmatian with different coloring. Racing across the slope and into the yard, they are a short bullet train, two sleek cars, close enough to appear attached. That they are still juveniles is clear from their lanky legs and their preference for prancing, galloping and trotting. Loki, in particular, reminds me of a colt.

In the five months between the puppies' arrival and my mother's death, my busyness with them, my sense of their beauty, their curiosity, and their intelligence, were forms of solace. I continued to work on things I valued, including editing a small online journal. But much of my energy was focused on things that were stressors—letter and postcard writing campaigns to influence the presidential election, mask-making for my family and friends with the hope of avoiding the COVID virus, and primarily the care of my mother, which became impossible in the last month of her life when we were no longer able to lift her. Though she had to go into a nursing home (where there were electronic patient lifts) in early November 2020, the care facility had opened up to visitors by that time, giving us peace of mind in the knowledge that among her five children, she would regularly have one of us there. She died on December 8, 2020.

More than a month previous to Zainy's death, I had an incident. It was January 6, 2020—the Epiphany and the first anniversary of my mother-in-law's death. A man, reminiscent of Ray Bradbury's Tattooed Man, shirtless in the cold winter night, fully inked with a half-circle tattoo covering his upper back, opened my front door and entered my house. I was sitting in the living room, reading, and didn't have my phone handy. Zainy was almost entirely deaf and slept soundly, The tattooed man walked down the hall and, feeling myself floating and time slowing, I saw that he didn't have a weapon in his hands. I called out to him, figuring that David, who was in the kitchen, would hear me and realize someone had entered. "What are you doing in my house?" I asked.

The man turned slowly and looked at me. "I was checking to see that everything was okay," he said. He seemed to be in his own fog, and I thought perhaps he had a mental disability.

"Well, here we are," I said.

"What does that mean?" he responded, agitated. Threatening, I thought.

David walked into the hallway, and seeing the man, stepped past him to the front door, opening it. "Thank you," he said. "We're fine, so you can go now." And, to my surprise, he did.

I later learned he was high, having shot up in my neighbors' yard. He had, in fact, been in more than one house on our street, and the police were on their way.

I think of this event as the birth of a constant anxiety that is only now abating. After that 2020 Epiphany visitation, I often felt my heart skipping beats while I drove home from my parents' residence, and had the sensation that if I didn't hold the steering wheel tight enough, I would float out of the car. Every semi truck that pulled left from the onramp into lanes of traffic made me feel that it would continue to skip lanes and smash into me. I knew this wasn't logical, and told myself so. Yet, this was my mind on stress and, later, on grief. This was the space I occupied.

During the pandemic shutdown, my cherished wilderness area was closed to visitors, then opened back up to masked visitors, and finally, opened without restrictions. I sometimes walked there alone, but only on the 'loop,' a fire road popular with hikers and bikers, more crowded than I liked. I'd grown afraid of walking alone in remote areas such as the one where Fletcher, Zainy, and I encountered the bear. I'd think of the strangeness of the tattooed man in my house and where else I might encounter him.

Yet I desired the wonder of moving through the wilderness again. When my sons visited, feeling safety in numbers, I'd have them join me and the pups in the hills, away from the crowded areas. I understand a new normal is at my heels—consistently asking for help. This isn't all bad.

In the midst of what I'd like to call a long drought, but what is probably another new normal, we had a night of rain. In the late morning, I sat in the backyard with the dogs to see how they liked the tail end of the storm, which had turned to a sprinkling. They weren't influenced by the drops much either way, although they both hate to be in water and will never have the pool fun that Zainy did. Once the rain had stopped completely, we decided to go out.

As we walked along the path, the dogs were alive to all the scents, heightened by the downpour. Thick in the humidity were jasmine and pine. Overarching all other scents was the powerful eucalyptus. While these trees explode in fires and are a particularly bad choice for a semi-arid environment, they were planted in the city long ago. In the moment, their glorious aroma was what I experienced. Loki and Curiosa held their heads high, stretched their necks.

I thought back to Zainy's adventures once she could no longer climb the slopes, the way she joyously scampered through piles of dry leaves on the same path we were then on. I, too, am aging out of the experiences I'd had with her and Fletcher. How long before I can no longer climb the slopes? Should I be lucky and live out a long life, I will continue on the downward trajectory I recently began with plantar fasciitis in my feet and the mild arthritis in my hips that causes long, fast walks to be painful. What will my experience with Loki and Curiosa be? If they live out their full lives, I will be seventy-five when they pass. I hope their rocket energy diminishes at a rate that keeps us in sync. Whatever happens, I know this: they are my last big dogs.

Dogs have taught me so many lessons over the years. Now that I have traveled the road of aging and death, not only with my pups, but with my parents, I have a pretty good idea what decreased activity means. If I can follow the examples of Fletcher and Zainy—continuing to push back against letting go of what I am able to do and gracefully accepting the challenges and the serendipity of each new stage of my life, each new normal, perhaps— just maybe—I can continue in joy.

But I'm not quite ready for the end of this important period of my life, and I promised myself to get past the anxiety and head out to the wilderness unaccompanied except for the dogs.

Though we climbed in a less traveled space, a group of hikers with dogs approached us from the opposite direction. One of the dogs pulled hard toward us, perhaps just interested, perhaps reactive or aggressive. As the man walking him was having some trouble, I decided to turn off on a thin line of a bike trail, one that connects back to the main path after a brief detour. Once away from the other group, we stopped to admire the meadow with its stand of live oaks.

It was in this very spot that Fletcher, Zainy, and I once watched a group of deer prance from one group of trees to another, nearly comic in seeming to hide. As I took in the blue sky, the tall waving grass, and the iridescent lizard absorbing Curiosa's attention, the past and present bloomed in me, both alive.

I stopped moving. Curiosa scanned the meadow, alert. We'd

been working to keep her from jumping on people when she's excited, but sensing the perfection of the moment, she raised herself on her hind legs and then reached upward with one paw, carefully setting it near my shoulder, as if to say, "Do you understand what's happening here?" Loki then joined her in tapping me.

And I do understand, am filled with awe for the beauty of our lives together in each particular moment.

ACKNOWLEDGMENTS

Thank you to Mark Givens, Dennis Callaci and Bamboo Dart Press for artwork, editorial advice, and nurturing this little chapbook into bloom. I love this series! Thanks to Laura DeKloe for her beautiful rendition of Zainy, which graces this cover. (Readers can find her work at https://laurajwd.wixsite.com/art-by-dekloe) Thanks to my Tuesday night writers workshop—Rachel, Linda, Jim, Jill, Chris, Randy, and Heather—for their help and advice as I wrote through the pandemic about life and loss.

ABOUT THE AUTHOR

Victoria Waddle is a Pushcart Prize-nominated writer, with fiction and nonfiction published in literary journals and anthologies, including in *Best Short Stories* from *The Saturday Evening Post Great American Fiction Contest*. A collection of her short fiction, *Acts of Contrition*, was published by Los Nietos Press. Formerly the managing editor of *Inlandia: A Literary Journey*, she helped to establish a yearly teen issue. In a previous life, she was a high school English teacher and librarian. The mother of three independent sons, she lives with her husband and two large, rambunctious rescue dogs in Southern California.

BAMBOO DART PRESS

112 N. Harvard Ave. #65
Claremont, CA 91711

chapbooks@bamboodartpress.com

www.bamboodartpress.com

CPSIA information can be obtained
at www.ICGtesting.com
Printed in the USA
BVHW021846240223
659186BV00008B/163